© 1990 Franklin Watts

First published in Great Britain
   1990 by
Franklin Watts
96 Leonard Street
London EC2A 4RH

First published in the USA by
Franklin Watts Inc
387 Park Avenue South
New York   NY 10016

First published in Australia by
Franklin Watts
14 Mars Road
Lane Cove
NSW 2066

UK ISBN: 0 7496 0210 4

Printed in Belgium

A CIP catalogue record for this
book is available from the British
Library

Designed by
K and Co

Photographs by
Angloco
Dennis Specialist Vehicles
Fire Department of New York
Surrey Fire Brigade
Merseyside Fire Brigade/Tony
   Myers
Simon Ladder Towers
Carmichael
Hong Kong Fire Services
Bell Helicopter Textron
Cleveland County Fire Brigade
London Fire Brigade
Longbeach 11th Coast Guard
FBM Marine
Hull Daily Mail

Technical Consultants
Amanda Brown
Mick France

The Picture World of

Fire Engines

Norman Barrett

CONTENTS

Franklin Watts

London • New York • Sydney • Toronto

Introduction

Fire engines rush firemen and fire fighting equipment to the scene of a fire. They have pumps and hoses to produce powerful jets of water. They carry ladders or platforms to help firemen reach the fire and for rescuing people who may be trapped.

There are many kinds of fire engines, used in different kinds of emergencies or for special purposes.

△ Firemen clamber over their fire engine during a drill, checking the equipment and practising their routines. This fire engine has a water tank with a powerful pump, several hoses and ladders of different lengths, as well as other equipment used for fire-fighting and rescue work.

▷ Some fire engines have ladder towers to lift firemen high off the ground.

▽ Firemen spray foam on an oil fire. Special materials such as foam and powders are used for fighting chemical, oil or petrol fires.

The front line

First at the scene of any incident are the basic fire engines. These are the water tenders and the aerial units.

Water tenders vary in size, depending on whether water is available from hydrants. They usually carry an extension ladder and other rescue equipment.

An aerial unit has an extension ladder mounted on a turntable. Another type has an elevating platform.

▽ Firemen tackle burning sugar and rubber in a warehouse fire. Several hoses may be attached to the pumps at the back of water tenders.

△ This aerial unit combines an extension ladder with an elevating platform. It is worked by hydraulic rams. The platform may be used for fire-fighting as well as rescue, water being obtained from a water tender or a hydrant. The ladders built into the extending arms may be used for continuous rescue. The whole unit is jacked up on four legs for stability.

◁ Fighting a building fire from an extension ladder.

▷ Firemen use a powerful water cannon, or monitor, to reach the heart of a fire.

▽ A jet of water is sprayed automatically from the top of a ladder as a fireman, in protective clothing and breathing apparatus, gets ready to move in.

△ An aerial unit with its turntable ladder retracted in transport position.

◁ Fighting a fire from an elevated platform.

Keeping control

A mobile control unit may be set up at major fires. This serves as an on-the-spot headquarters.

Most large control units have separate sections. They have a communications room, with field telephones and radio, for co-ordinating the whole operation.

They carry detailed maps of the area, floor plans of buildings and other local information. There is also space for senior officers to have meetings.

▽ A mobile control unit. Inside, it is divided into sections for various purposes.

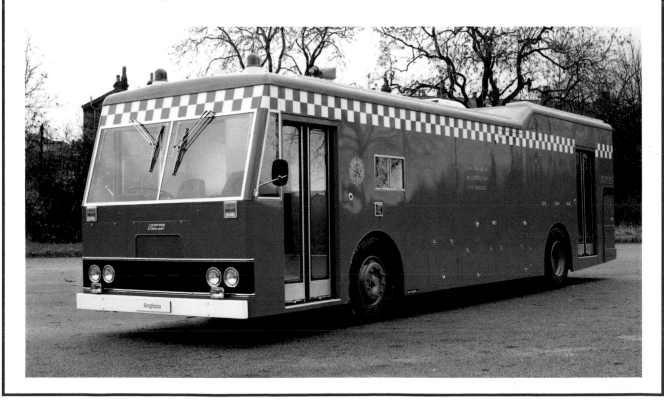

Specialist and support vehicles

Some types of fire engines are designed to do special jobs, such as fighting forest fires. Other tenders arrive at the scene to support the main water tenders and aerial units.

Support vehicles include water tankers and vehicles carrying emergency generators or other equipment. At major incidents, a canteen van might be set up to provide meals for the firemen.

▽ Water tankers are brought in when there is no water available from hydrants or rivers. This one carries nearly 7,000 litres (1,500 gall).

△ A forest fire-fighting appliance. It has all-wheel drive and chunky tyres for travelling over rough or muddy ground, a crane for removing obstacles such as fallen trees, and a water tank with a portable pump.

▷ An emergency tender with electric generators that slide out on trays. Other equipment carried includes winches, cutting gear and breathing apparatus.

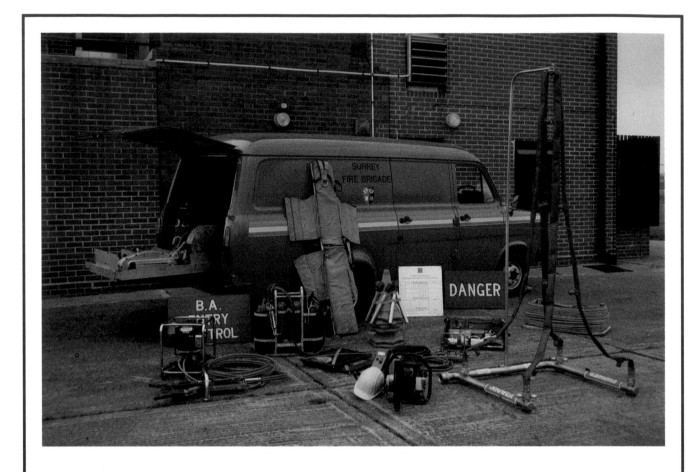

△ An emergency accident vehicle carries equipment likely to be needed at a crash. This includes motor-powered cutting gear (left) and a portable shower unit (right) so that fire-fighters can wash off any dangerous substances.

◁ A breathing apparatus van which can carry extra cylinders of compressed air.

Containing danger

Among the most difficult fires to tackle are those involving dangerous substances such as chemicals or oil. Special vehicles and equipment are needed, and the firemen wear special protective clothing.

Foam is used to smother oil or petrol fires or to prevent them starting. Water would be dangerous, because it spreads the flammable substance more widely.

▽ A light refinery fire tender based on a small van conversion. Some companies have their own chemical incident units (CIUs). This one contains a tank with pre-mixed foam, suction hose for drawing up water, ladders, and breathing apparatus.

◁ Firemen dressed in chemical protective suits in front of a decontamination unit. Here they can be sprayed down to get rid of dangerous chemicals.

▽ An airport fire truck shoots foam from a monitor at the top. Foam tenders either carry the foam or make it by mixing a special compound with water.

Rescue tenders

Fire engines are used for other emergencies as well as fires. In many countries they operate as the main rescue service. They may be needed for pumping away flood water or freeing people trapped in collapsed buildings or wrecked vehicles.

Special rescue or emergency tenders may be sent to incidents where rescue equipment such as heavy cutting gear is needed.

△ The tiller rig, used in the United States, is really two vehicles coupled together. It swivels in the middle, enabling it to negotiate sharp corners and busy city traffic. It is driven from the front, with another driver at the back to steer the back section. It provides long extension ladders on a turntable for rescuing people from high buildings.

19

△ A rescue tender with floodlights on an extended mast and with portable lighting.

▷ An aerial ladder is used across a river for a rescue operation.

◁ A rescue tender stands by while firemen put out a vehicle fire after a motor accident.

21

▷ A light rescue tender showing the stowage of some of its equipment. This includes cutting gear, hand tools, and a first aid kit.

▽ A heavy, four-wheel-drive rescue tender with a winch mounted at the front. The winch is used mainly for hauling vehicles out of trouble.

Fire boats and helicopters

Some fires may be reached only by air or water. Fire boats are used at large dock areas or in wide rivers. They fight fires on ships or in waterfront buildings. Helicopters help to fight forest or bush fires.

Fire boats have pumps that draw water from rivers or seas. The larger, seagoing vessels might have hospital cabins and be equipped with hydraulic platforms. The largest fire boats are operated by oil companies.

▽ Fire boats in action in Hong Kong Harbour. They can spray water or foam.

△ Fire boats move in to tackle a fire on board an oil tanker.

◁ A fire boat demonstrates its powerful jets.

▽ A helicopter drops chemicals to stop a bush fire from spreading. Water may also be dropped to put out forest fires. Some helicopters scoop up water from the sea or lakes in huge buckets.

Facts

The first fire appliances

Fire has always been a dangerous hazard, and the first known fire engine was invented more than 2,000 years ago in ancient Greece. It was a device that used twin pumps to produce a continuous jet of water.

But mechanical fire-fighting equipment fell into disuse. It was another 1,600 years before inventors again turned their attentions to designing fire engines. The first steam-powered pump was built in London in 1829.

△ A skid unit for mounting in a suitable pick-up truck. It has a 270 litre (60 gall) water tank. Other features include a flashing beacon, a siren and a searchlight.

Saving space

Small self-contained fire engine units have been designed for mounting in pick-up trucks. Called skid units, they have a petrol-driven pump, a water tank, and suction hose for drawing from open water.

On tracks

Some cross-country fire trucks run on tracks, like a tank. These are the best type of ground vehicles for tackling grass or bush fires spread over a large area. While helicopters are valuable in getting fire-fighters and equipment quickly to out-

△ Firemen of the London Fire Brigade demonstrate a horse-drawn steam-powered pump first used more than 100 years ago.

△ A fire and rescue unit of the type used by the Royal Air Force in the Falkland Islands. Tracked vehicles can tackle any type of terrain. This unit contains a large foam tank and all the necessary fire-fighting and rescue equipment.

of-the way places, there is a limit to the amount of water they can carry.

Starting fires

Some fire engines have been built to start fires! Strange as this may seem, one method of halting the spread of bush and forest fires is to burn up an area in front of the fire. The vehicle carries a fire retardant material which is sprayed along a line in the path of the fire. A fire is then started in the direction of the approaching flames, so that there is nothing left to burn. As a result, the forest or bush fire burns itself out.

Inflatable dinghies

Among the smallest fire boats are the inflatable rubber dinghies that serve as inshore fire and rescue units in some places. No more than about 4 m (13 ft) long, they are capable of speeds of more than 35 knots (65 km/h or 40 mph). They may operate from larger fire boats, and are used to speed to the incident and pick up any victims. They carry portable fire-fighting equipment when necessary.

△ A Searider inflatable dinghy of the Cleveland County Fire Brigade, in northern England, on its way to an incident. Apart from its crew of two, it can carry 10 passengers.

Glossary

Decontamination
Removing all traces of dangerous substances from firemen and equipment after a chemical fire.

Elevating platform
An open platform or cage at the end of an extending arm that can be raised up from a fire engine.

Fire-retardant
Any substance or material that slows the spread of fire or prevents it starting.

Flammable
A flammable substance is one that will burn.

Foam
A lather used for smothering fires. Foam is used when water by itself would be dangerous.

Hydrant
A connection for attaching a hose to a water main or similar source of water.

Hydraulic ram
A cylinder operated by liquid pressure and used to manoeuvre elevating platforms.

Ladder tower
A ladder raised mechanically from a fire engine.

Monitor
A device for spraying materials such as foam at high pressure.

Suction hose
Hose used for drawing up open water, as from a river or lake.

Tiller rig
A fire engine made of two vehicles coupled together, with a driver at the back as well as the front.

Water tender
A fire engine whose chief purpose is to carry and pump water.

Winch
A device that uses a rope wound round a drum to haul vehicles or hoist weights.

Index